Do You Know?

ABOUT

CASTLES AND CRUSADERS

By
Philip Sauvain
Illustrated by
Jim Robins

Warwick Press
New York/Toronto
1986

Contents

About 1,500 years ago, the mighty Roman Empire was destroyed by hordes of invaders.

The fall of the Roman Empire marks the start of the 1,000-year period we call the Middle Ages, or medieval age. It was a troubled time for the people of Europe. Even when many of the invaders had settled into a more peaceful way of life, there were still long and violent wars between rival countries. The "feudal system" meant that a few people were very rich and powerful, while hundreds of peasants lived and worked like slaves.

However, many towns grew up and great castles and cathedrals were built during this time. And by the end of the Middle Ages a new age of exploration and discovery had begun.

wm
J
w m q q v E
940.18
Sau

ISBN 531-19015-3

Library of Congress Catalog Card No. 85-52277

Published 1986 by Warwick Press, 387 Park Avenue South, New York, New York 10016.
First published in 1986 by Piper Books Ltd., London.
Copyright © by Piper Books Ltd., 1986
Printed in Spain.
5 4 3 2 1

1 Raiders and Invaders

The Romans brought order and civilization to the lands they conquered. In countries like Britain, they built fine roads and houses like the ones in their own country. Their strong armies kept the fierce Scots and Picts at bay in the north, and discouraged attacks from raiders across the sea.

However, tribes of Goths and Vandals from northern Europe were attacking other parts of the Roman Empire. As the invaders moved nearer and nearer to Italy, every Roman soldier was needed at home to defend his country. A warrior named Alaric eventually led his tribe of Visigoths into Rome, setting many buildings on fire. Romans fled through the streets in terror as the raiders stole treasure from their homes.

The fiercest of all the invaders were the Huns from central Asia. Under their leader, Attila, they were to drive many of the other raiders out of their own lands into those of the Roman Empire.

In the meantime, the people of Britain were left to the mercy of their enemies. Scots and Picts poured south across the border, while the Angles, Saxons and Jutes sailed from Germany to make raids along the coast.

In time, the raiders returned to settle in Britain. They lived in family groups in villages, ruled by the chief of the tribe. They were good farmers, and skilled at plowing even the hardest soil.

Some Romans moved to the old Greek city of Byzantium, which they called Constantinople after the Emperor Constantine. Constantine was a Christian. His influence can be seen in the religious art of the time.

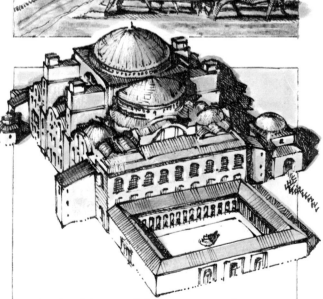

The buildings of Constantinople were in the Roman style. The huge cathedral of St. Sophia at Constantinople was built to the orders of the Emperor Justinian — the greatest of the Byzantine emperors.

② Emperor Charlemagne

By about A.D. 700 (700 years after the birth of Christ), most of the invading tribes had settled down. Europe became divided into a number of countries ruled by Christian kings.

The greatest king in Europe at this time was Charlemagne, the leader of the Franks. Charlemagne was so successful in battle that by the end of his reign he controlled huge areas of Europe, including what is now France, Germany, the Netherlands, Italy, and northern Spain. He was a wise and far-seeing ruler, who encouraged education in the schools and monasteries. He also built churches in the lands he conquered, which pleased the Pope very much. In A.D. 800 he crowned Charlemagne "Holy Roman Emperor."

Charlemagne ruled by the "feudal system." This was the main system of government in Europe at this time. At the top of the system was the king himself. Everybody in the land owed loyalty to the king. Next came the nobles, who swore oaths of loyalty to the throne and promised to come to the king's aid if he went to war. In return for these services, the nobles were given control over large areas of land. This might include several farming villages.

The nobles built castles to defend their land, and supported their own army of soldiers. Their estates were often divided into manors, which were run by less important lords. Much of the farming land of the manor was shared out among the peasants. In return for their strips of land, the peasants had to work without wages for the lord for part of the week, and also at harvest time. They also had to give him some of the crops they grew.

The lords kept a firm control over their peasants' private lives. If they broke the law, the lord was the judge. If they wished to marry, the lord had to give his approval first. And they could only leave their villages with his agreement. In many ways, most medieval peasants were little more than slaves.

(3) The Vikings

Just to the north of Charlemagne's empire lay the lands of the Vikings. These northern people became famous for their skill as sea voyagers and were feared for their warlike nature.

Sailing from Denmark and Norway in their long wooden ships, the Vikings made fierce raids along the coast of Europe. Many attacks were on the Christian monasteries. These were easy targets for the sea robbers, being rich with jewels and gold, and often guarded only by a few helpless monks.

Jorvik

Countries like England and France suffered a lot from the searaiders. Soon, the Vikings made more daring raids inland, sailing up rivers in their narrow boats. Riding across the country on stolen horses, the Vikings stole and killed, and burned whole villages to the ground. In Britain, they took many Saxon farmers as slaves and forced whole areas to pay them protection money, known as "Danegeld."

In time, some Vikings returned to seize land for themselves. In England, they forced the Saxons into the west and took over the east part of the country. They built prosperous towns, such as Jorvik (York) in the northeast. Merchants from all over Europe came to trade at Jorvik.

Other Vikings settled in France. It was a descendant of these northern men (Normans) who was later to become the last raider to overthrow Britain, in 1066.

Viking farm

Although we usually think of the Vikings as fierce raiders, many were simply farmers. It was mainly the lack of good farming land at home that drove so many Vikings abroad to other lands. This is one of the reasons why they became such skilled boat-builders and explorers.

The Vikings traveled amazing distances in search of new farming land. As well as sailing all around Europe, some reached as far as Greenland and North America. We know a lot about these seamen's lives from stories, called sagas, which tell of great kings who were buried at sea. The funeral ship was laden with treasure and all the food and wine the king might need in his "after-life." Then the boat was set alight, and sent to drift out to sea ablaze.

4 The Norman Conquest

When King Edward of England died in 1066, Duke William, the leader of the Normans, claimed the English throne was his by right of a promise made by the old king. On hearing that the people of England had chosen a noble called Harold to be their king instead, William gathered his armies for an invasion.

In October of the same year, the Normans crossed the Channel and landed in the south of England. They were met by Harold and his army of Saxons. In a day-long battle the Norman knights, many of whom were on horseback, charged the Saxon footsoldiers. The fighting was fierce, but the day ended in triumph for the Normans.

Norman knight

Saxon noble

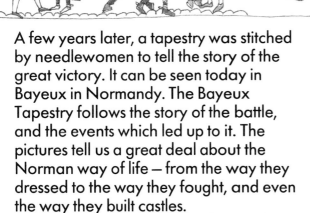

A few years later, a tapestry was stitched by needlewomen to tell the story of the great victory. It can be seen today in Bayeux in Normandy. The Bayeux Tapestry follows the story of the battle, and the events which led up to it. The pictures tell us a great deal about the Norman way of life — from the way they dressed to the way they fought, and even the way they built castles.

In the part of the tapestry shown above, the death of Harold is shown in pictures, while the Latin writing reads "Harold the king is killed." Further scenes show the Normans riding to victory while the Saxons fled to their homes.

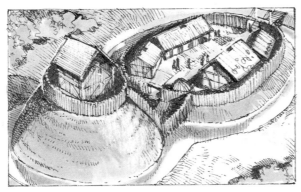

After Hastings, William built castles all over England to protect his knights against the Saxons. These early castles were simple wooden towers built on raised mounds of earth. A strong fence around the tower and another one lower down kept enemies out, but it was a rather uncomfortable home.

In 1086, William sent officials to find out exactly what was happening in his country. He wanted to know what taxes people were paying. He also ordered his officials to count the livestock and to record the size of the fields in every manor in the country. This famous survey became known as the Domesday Book.

5 A Medieval Village

Most medieval peasants knew very little about life outside their own small village. Since they grew or made everything they needed to live on, there was no real need to travel — in fact, to do so without the lord of the manor's permission was strictly forbidden.

A typical village was made up of twenty or thirty little huts made of wicker and mud. The lord's manor house was the center of law, but the church was the heart of village life. There might also be a well, a forge, an alehouse, and maybe a windmill for grinding corn into flour. Some peasants became craftsmen or blacksmiths, but most spent their days toiling in the fields. The most important time of the year was the harvest. If the crops failed, it would mean a hungry winter.

In the winter the soil was turned over by plows which were pulled by teams of oxen (cattle). The peasant's wife used a long stick to poke them with if they plodded along too slowly.

The spring was sowing time. The sower held the sack of seed under his arm and spread it over the soil. Boys used slings to hurl stones at the birds if they tried to eat the seed on the ground.

In the late summer the crop was cut. Men and women used sharp iron blades (called sickles) to cut the stalks of wheat. These were then put in bundles and carted back to the village.

In the fall the wheat was thrashed with flails. These were sticks which knocked the ears away from the stalks. Then the ears were thrown in the air to let the wind blow bits of straw away.

Later on in the fall the sacks of wheat were taken to the mill to be ground into flour. In some villages this was a windmill on a hill. In other villages it was a watermill on a nearby river.

Christmas was a holy day (holiday). The peasants put up holly in the great hall of the manor house. A burning yule log kept the peasants warm as they ate a big feast and drank jugs of ale.

6 Life In A Monastery

Not all manors were owned by nobles and knights. Many belonged to the abbeys and priories, run by monks and nuns. Abbeys run by monks were called monasteries, while those run by nuns were known as nunneries.

Monks and nuns led a simple life of prayer, study, and hard work. They owned no personal possessions, and lived by a set of strict rules. Their first duty was to God, and much of the day was taken up with saying prayers. The abbey church was always a splendid building, many being as big as a cathedral.

In between prayers, there were countless household chores to be done. Many abbeys had large farms, where monks and nuns grew vegetables and kept sheep and cattle. They also caught fish in the abbey pond, kept bees for honey and candlewax, and made medicines and ointment from herbs. Many baked their own bread and brewed their own ale. Some monks also worked as carpenters or blacksmiths.

The first prayer service began long before daybreak. After this, the monks and nuns returned to bed until dawn. There were six other services during the day.

After a light breakfast, the monks and nuns gathered in the chapter house. A chapter of the abbey rules was read, and the everyday business of the abbey was discussed.

Although their day began so early, it was usually past noon when they had their main meal. They were not allowed to talk, but there was usually a reading from the Bible.

Monks and nuns also played an important part in everyday life outside the abbey. They gave money, clothes, and food to the poor, and offered hospitality to travelers. They also cared for the sick, as there were no hospitals in those days in any countries in Europe.

There were very few schools or universities in the Middle Ages. The monks were among the few people who could read and write, so the monasteries became great centers of learning. As well as teaching children, they spent hours copying books by hand onto pieces of parchment. Using pens made from feathers, they painted beautiful pictures on every page. These pictures help us to understand what life in the Middle Ages was like.

(7) Defending a Castle

Kings and the more powerful nobles lived in castles rather than manor houses. At first these were simple wooden towers, but later on much stronger castles were built out of stone.

Thick walls surrounded the inner courtyard. Here stood the square tower, or keep, where the people of the castle lived. Long slits were built into the walls, so that archers could fire arrows at soldiers attacking the castle without being hit themselves. Gaps at the top of the walls allowed them to hurl missiles at the enemy below.

The walls were often surrounded by a deep ditch called a moat, sometimes filled with water. Normally people crossed the moat by means of the drawbridge, but if an enemy was sighted then the guards quickly cranked it up on heavy chains. The spiked iron door could then be slammed down across the entrance.

Soldiers attacking a castle would often try to starve their enemy into surrender. They settled down in camps outside the castle walls, and prevented anyone from delivering food or other supplies. This was called a siege.

Breaking into a castle by force was a much more dangerous task. Some of the attackers would dig tunnels into the courtyard, or climb the walls using long ladders. As they did so, the defenders poured boiling water or heavy boulders onto their heads.

Missiles were hurled against the walls by huge siege catapults while other soldiers set up a battering ram. This was a large tree trunk, which swung from ropes attached to a wooden frame. The frame was covered by leather, to shield the soldiers from arrows raining down from the castle walls. The ram was swung against the castle gate, until finally it gave way.

8 A Castle Home

Great Hall   Kitchen   Solar

Many people lived in a medieval castle. As well as the lord and his family, servants of all ranks and ages bustled about their duties. Visiting noblemen and royal messengers were received and entertained, and peasants from the surrounding countryside came to pay their rent.

The great hall was the social center of the castle, where everyone dined together. Many cooks, bakers, and dairy-maids were kept busy in the kitchen preparing food for such large numbers. At night, the soldiers and servants slept on the drafty stone floor of the hall, while the lord and his lady retired to their private room. This was called the solar.

In case of attack, the castle had to be well stocked with weapons. This was the job of the armorer. He also had to repair the soldiers' metal tunics, and keep their swords sharp.

Armoury

18

When they were not at war, nobles loved to hunt on the castle estate. Whole forests were often set aside as royal hunting grounds for the king and his nobles.

One of the favorite ways of hunting was with hawks and falcons. These were specially trained to attack small animals and birds. Noble ladies also enjoyed this sport. Huntsmen were in charge of the hounds, which were used to chase deer and wild boars.

Tournaments (mock battles) were often held at the castle at holiday time. The atmosphere was rather like a fair, with many colorful tents and the fanfare of trumpets.

The most exciting part was the joust. Two armored knights galloped at each other on brightly-dressed horses. Using a blunt wooden lance, they tried to unseat each other from their mounts. Knights were sometimes seriously injured, but the victor won great honor and the favor of his lady.

In the Middle Ages, many romantic ballads were sung about knights who were honest and merciful, as well as gallant and brave. But real life was not always like the songs. Some knights were brutal and cruel, seizing lands and goods which did not belong to them and killing anyone who stood in their way.

At one siege, women, children and old men were thrown out of the castle at night by their own soldiers. The knights inside did not want to waste their scarce food and water on people who could not defend the castle. When King Richard the Lionheart of England eventually starved one town into surrender after a long siege, he killed 3,000 prisoners in cold blood although they had bravely defended their home for many weeks.

A knight leaving for war in his battle armor was an impressive sight. His horse would be robed in rich cloth, and his shield painted brightly in his "coat of arms" — the emblem of the noble family he belonged to.

Longbow

Crossbow

War in the Middle Ages often ended in death or terrible injuries. Arms, noses, and heads were cut off by axes and swords, and arrows pierced eyes and mouths.

Soldiers fought with two main types of weapon. There were those which could be held in the hand, such as swords, clubs, spiked poles, and axes. There were also missiles which could be thrown or hurled at the enemy, such as stones and arrows.

Arrows from the deadly English longbow flew faster and farther than those from the crossbow favored by the French army. At the battle of Crécy in 1346, English archers fired their arrows from behind a fence of wooden stakes, piercing the armor of the mounted French knights a hundred yards away. The French army was defeated long before they could get near the English soldiers.

War was always flaring up between France and England at this time. In 1428, English soldiers surrounded the French town of Orléans. For many months they attacked the city with cannons and huge catapults. The war leader who ended the siege was a young peasant girl called Joan of Arc. She convinced the French leaders that religious "voices" had commanded her to lead the French army against the English. The French troops took fresh hope from her faith, and in 1428 they beat the enemy into retreat.

⑩ Islam And The Crusades

In the Middle East, the world had changed since the days of Jesus Christ and the Romans. A new religion spread across north Africa and Arabia. This was Islam — the religion of the Muslims.

The founder of Islam was the prophet Mohammed. Muslims believe that Mohammed was visited by an angel, who taught him God's commands. These commands were later written down in the Holy Book of Islam—the Koran. Islam spread quickly, as the Muslims conquered lands as far west as Spain and Portugal. The Muslims built fine mosques and palaces all over their empire. Their houses often faced inward onto shady courtyards, and the walls were plastered white to keep them cool. You can always recognize a Muslim city from its brightly colored roofs with round domes. In Spain, Muslim buildings can still be seen in towns like Granada and Seville.

Muslim traders carried goods from one end of the empire to the other. They traveled on camels and donkeys, roped together in processions called caravans. Many traders dealt in luxuries — gold and ivory from Africa, silk and spices from the Far East, and furs from northeast Europe.

Many Muslims were peaceful people. But one group, the Saracens, were fierce fighters who tried to turn other nations into Muslims by force. When they seized the holy city of Jerusalem nearly a thousand years ago, the Pope called on Christian kings everywhere to fight against Islam in the Holy Land.

Knights from many different countries banded against the common enemy. They called their campaign a "crusade" (a "war of the cross") and they wore the sign of the cross on their armor.

The Crusaders won many victories, and for a long time they managed to defend Jerusalem. They built huge castles, and provided shelter for many Christian pilgrims. However, after nearly a hundred years of war, the Saracens forced them to leave. The knights were never to capture the city again.

Muslim scientists were among the greatest in the world, and their doctors were more skilled than any in Europe. In astronomy (the study of stars and planets), their invention of the astrolabe helped sailors to find their way by watching the stars.

The Muslims were also great teachers. Throughout the Empire, people were taught Arabic so that they could read the Koran. In mathematics, their system of counting (1, 2, 3, etc., unlike the Roman I, II, III) is still in use today.

Numbers 1—9
Astrolabe
Koran

⑪ The Medieval World

Constantinople

Today, historians have made it possible for us to find out how people lived in many parts of the world in the Middle Ages. However, the people living in Europe at this time knew nothing of the great civilizations that flourished in America, and little about those in the East.

The people in western Europe did know about the great Byzantine empire at Constantinople. Merchants brought back many luxury goods, until the war in the Holy Land made trading difficult. However, the riches of the Far East were not discovered until the Italian traveler Marco Polo crossed to China in about 1275.

Neither the Europeans nor the Asians knew that the huge continent of America existed. Yet in Peru 500 years ago the Inca people had built a great empire. Their skilled craft workers made many beautiful gold ornaments. In Mexico, the Aztec city of Tenochtitlan was one of the largest and most splendid in the world. It was built on an island reached by bridges, and there were many temples, fine buildings and huge pyramids in the city. It had a good system of water supply, and its streets were kept clean by professional road sweepers.

Mexico

Peru

Tenochtitlan

Mongol caravan

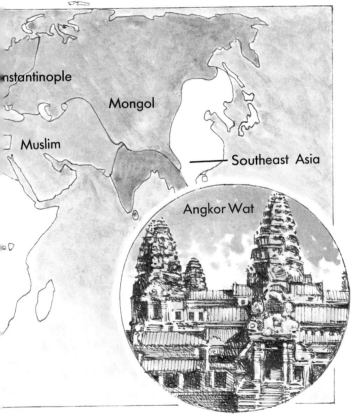

Constantinople

Mongol

Muslim

Southeast Asia

Angkor Wat

Samarkand

There were also great civilizations in the Far East during the Middle Ages. In southeast Asia, the people who lived in what is now called Vietnam built a huge temple at a place called Angkor Wat. Much of their way of life was influenced by the great Chinese empire.

Eight hundred years ago, most of Asia was conquered by Genghis Khan, the king of the Mongols. The Mongols were wandering tribes who traveled the flat, treeless plains of central Asia in search of grazing land. They traveled in caravans, taking their round tentlike homes with them — on wheels!

The Mongols were a tough and warlike people. Ghenghiz Khan's fierce army of horsemen could fire their bows with deadly effect, even when riding at full speed.

Ghenghiz Khan seized a huge empire, from China in the east to Hungary in the west. His methods of war were merciless. At the siege of Samarkand, prisoners were used as human shields while his warriors set the city ablaze.

25

⑫ City Life

The streets of European towns in the Middle Ages were not as clean as those of Tenochtitlan. Towns like Venice, Florence, Bruges, London, Hamburg, Nuremberg, and Paris were dirty and crowded with people. Many had strong walls around them to protect the people of the town from attack. At night the town gates were shut and armed soldiers were put on guard.

The narrow streets of the towns were often made of earth. Pigs and chickens ran in the streets. There were very few drains and water pipes in those days. Instead, an open gutter running with filth often ran through the middle of the street.

People got their water from a well or river. Many buildings had thatched roofs, so the risk of fire was great. Most houses were small and cramped, and very few had gardens. Although some towns had space for small farms, most town dwellers relied on country people to bring fresh food to market each day.

Markets and fairs were held in the town's squares, and shops were built along the narrow streets in the center. Streets were often named after these shops, such as Butcher Row and Baker Street.

The goods they sold were made in private houses. The craftsmen who made them were members of groups called guilds, run by each type of trader. The guilds trained young men in their chosen craft, as well as making sure that the standard of work was high among all its members. The bakers had a guild, as did the butchers and the leather workers. Each guild had its own rules. They elected a master and built a meeting place called the guildhall. Many of these guildhalls can be seen today.

The members of the guilds sometimes acted in "mystery" plays based on stories from the bible. These were performed on stages called pageants, which were built on wheels so that they could be moved around the town. They often took place on special religious occasions, and they aimed not only to entertain but to teach their audience a moral lesson. Crowds gathered eagerly to listen, sometimes jeering loudly at the performers! The stories the guildsmen acted were often chosen because they were about the jobs done by their members. The carpenters might put on a play about Noah building the ark. Seamen told the story of Jonah and the Whale.

Seamen could be seen in many of the great ports of the Middle Ages. Merchants from all parts of Europe came to do business with those of other countries.

(13) Exploring The World

The end of the Middle Ages was also the beginning of a great new age of exploration and discovery. The main reason behind the sea voyages of the great explorers was the need to find a new route to the East.

In the 1200s, the Italian explorer Marco Polo crossed Asia by land and spent many years in China. On his return, people were amazed by his tales of the spices and jewels to be found in the Far East. Merchants eager to make a profit soon followed his route, buying cargoes of spices which could be sold for very high prices in Europe. However, there was a problem. By 1400 the land route to the Far East had become too risky, since the way was blocked by fierce tribes of Muslims and Mongols.

Henry the Navigator

Some thought that the best way to reach India and China by sea was to sail round southern Africa. In Portugal, Prince Henry the Navigator sent seamen from Lisbon to explore the African coast. To help his sailors, Henry brought together his most skilled mapmakers, astronomers, pilots, and ship designers.

Lisbon

Two of Portugal's most famous explorers were Bartholomew Diaz and Vasco da Gama. In 1485 Bartholomew Diaz became the first European to sail as far as the Cape of Good Hope, the most southerly point in Africa. Twelve years later Vasco da Gama set sail from Lisbon with four ships. After reaching the Cape of Good Hope he sailed up the eastern coast of Africa. From there he hired an Arab pilot to show him the way to India. He reached the Indian coast in 1498, where he collected cargoes of spices and jewels.

Da Gama's voyage opened up the first sea route to the Far East. However, the journey cost the lives of three-fourths of his ships' crew.

The voyage of Vasco da Gama

North America
Portugal
India
Africa
South America
Columbus
Da Gama

Meanwhile, another famous seaman tried to reach the Far East by sailing in the opposite direction across the Atlantic Ocean. Christopher Columbus set sail from Spain in 1492. His three ships were the *Nina*, the *Pinta* and the *Santa Maria*. When he reached the islands of the Caribbean in central America he thought he had landed in India. This is why the islands he saw were called the West Indies, and why the people there and on the mainland became known as "Indians."

Vasco da Gama and Christopher Columbus were followed by many other seamen and explorers. The exploration of the world had begun.

(14) Inventions and Discoveries

The voyages of discovery came at a time when the people living in Europe were eager to find out as much as they could about the world. They took a fresh interest in discovering what the Greeks and Romans had learned more than a thousand years earlier. It was this which gave rise to the age we call the Renaissance (meaning "rebirth").

There were also many new inventions. These included spectacles, gunpowder, and the printing press. The first person to print books was a German called Johannes Gutenberg, in 1440. By 1476, William Caxton had begun printing books in Britain from his printing press in London.

Before then, only a few people had been able to read the hand-written manuscripts produced by the monks. The printing press meant that cheap books could be bought and read by thousands of people. Books could also be written for children to use in school, and so helped education to spread.

Up until this time, artists and sculptors had produced rather flat and stiff-looking works. By studying the art of a thousand years earlier, they learned to create paintings and sculptures which looked lifelike. Builders also copied Greek and Roman styles, combining the columns and pillars of the Greek style of architecture with the graceful domes and arches of the Roman buildings.

Great centers of learning had sprung up at monasteries and universities in Europe. Some of the subjects studied were frowned upon by religious leaders. For example, many discoveries made in astronomy went against the teachings of the Church. The science of alchemy (an attempt to change cheap metals into gold or silver by means of chemistry) was also disapproved of.

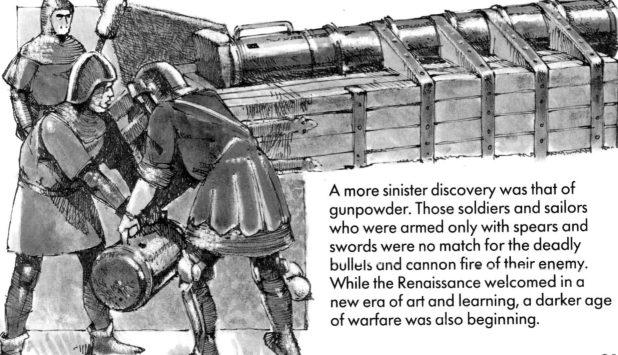

A more sinister discovery was that of gunpowder. Those soldiers and sailors who were armed only with spears and swords were no match for the deadly bullets and cannon fire of their enemy. While the Renaissance welcomed in a new era of art and learning, a darker age of warfare was also beginning.

31

Index